Shampoo

Shampoo

BY: ARIEL SARA R.

Illustrations by Daisy Murray

SHAMPOO

www.ArielSaraR.com

ISBN: 978-0-9983324-3-7

Illustrations by: Daisy Murray

Second edition 2016

Dedication

For those
with endless wonder in their eyes

And for those
who are miserably hurting
yet seek to rise

Don't give up,
I hear your cries

Wash your hair & cleanse your soul
Come back to yourself

Remember that
You were born complete
Remember that
You are whole

This is for you—

~ ARIEL SARA R.

Introduction

Shampoo is split into four cleansing cycles—each a vital component to the full experience of a hair-and-soul cleanse.

Baby Shampoo *is for soft and sensitive hair, enabling the soul to innocently experience falling in love.*

Shampoo For Damaged Hair *is appropriate for hair that has endured severe damage, as well as for treating heart-broken souls.*

Detangler gets rid of knots in the hair, along with allowing a soothing release of tension in the soul.

Shampoo For Extra Shine *adds a radiant glow to each strand of hair, while building strength in the individuality of one's soul.*

Feel free to rinse and repeat as desired!

She takes off her crown
and enters the shower
Freed from pretty people with ugly power

Warm water trickles down,
No need for a fancy gown

Feeling caged for weeks,
the mascara runs down her cheeks
Young and unique,
Positivity is all she seeks

She has a world of her own
Sings melodies with a magical tone

She runs the ***shampoo*** through her hair
Cold-hearted, without the slightest care.

~ Ariel Sara R.

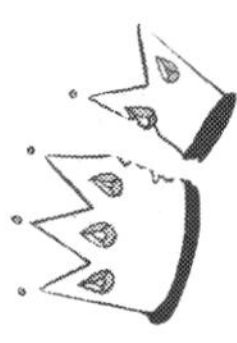

Table of Contents

Baby Shampoo

Baby Shampoo

(For **soft** and **sensitive** hair)

- *Tear-free*
- *For young and pure hearts*
- *Gentle to the eyes and soul*
- *For innocent souls only*

WARNING: Do not leave in product for too long. Consequences may include split ends and broken hearts.

When I see you, I lose my sense of self-control
I let the wondrous feeling encompass my soul
All I want is to gaze at your flaws all day
and I don't care the slightest bit that it's cliché

You're all that I desire
My heart is burning,
and I can't hide the fire

Look me in the eyes
Tell me how you feel
Let's keep turning this crazy love wheel

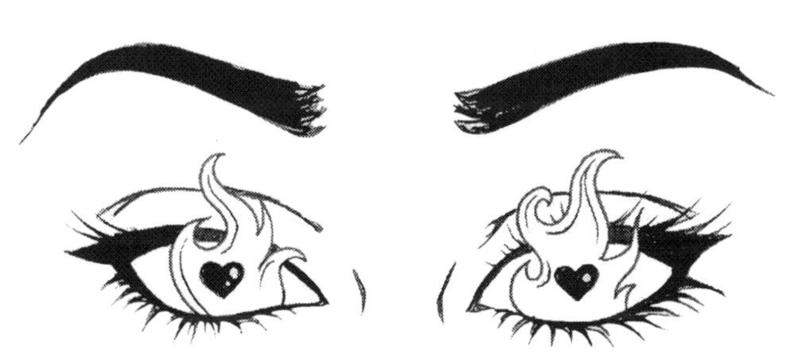

You own my heart and you don't even know
This is becoming dangerous
So please, let's take it slow

Whisper your secrets in my ear
Every time you leave, I'm filled with fear

Whatever you do,
please stay near

I need you now,
I need you here

Your voice makes me fall asleep
not that it's boring
but it takes me to a land so far away
with no tomorrow and no yesterday

It makes me feel secure,
righteous, and perfectly pure

Your secret smile is showing
along with those big beautiful eyes,
glowing

My love for you is
helplessly overflowing

and my addiction for you
is explosively growing

I see you from afar,
giving me a special glance

I hope that means
we have a chance

I'm just tired of waiting for you to advance

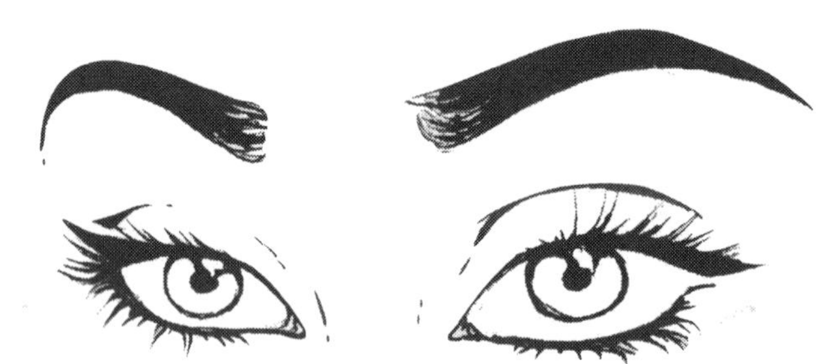

I can see us in the moonlight
Serenaded,
ready to dance

I feel our energies gracefully collide
I can see us together,
side by side

Your eyes paint a universe
that I dream of living in

I recognize your smile
I've seen it in my dreams

The way it lights up the room
and even
the way it screams.

My heart began telling a tale
but my mind lifted the veil

The battle continued
Love or *logic?*

My heart screams forward
as my mind holds me back

My past builds walls
And my future breaks them all

I leap with courage
but cry with fear
Hesitation floods my veins
as I pull the trigger of risk,

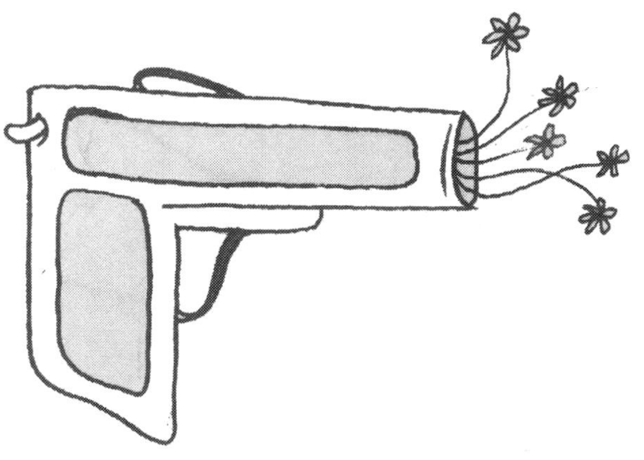

hoping that reward awaits me

I'm at a loss for words
when you come in the room

You radiate so bright,
the sun must get jealous

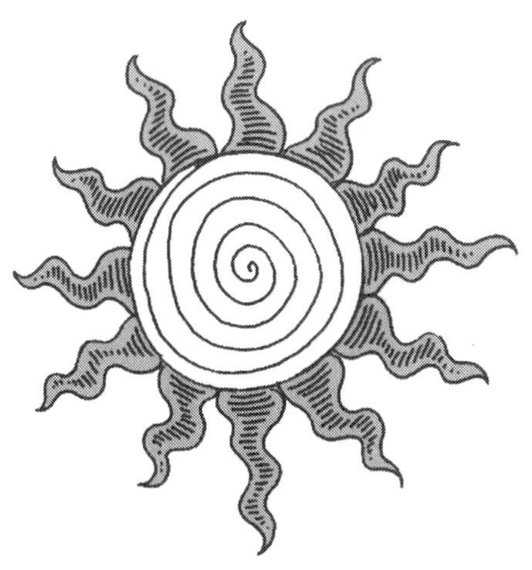

because you stole her light
without a fight
and
just wore it as a casual smile

I'm scared for our eyes to meet
because I know
that the second you see mine

you'll know how much I want you
and take me for granted

We are so perfectly ugly in our own unique, wicked way.

Cold shoulder,
with a mysterious smile

I can't figure you out.

Playing quiet…
but something tells me you want to shout

Please tell me what this is all about
Your twisted ways
are leaving me with doubt

I recognized you right away

The shyness screams from your eyes
so I don't need to listen
to what you cannot say

as this strange outcast
that you portray

I cannot tell if this is a game
but my heart wants to play
Just need to convince my mind to obey

Now that we're on a roll
Just tell me when to fold

And through thick and thin,

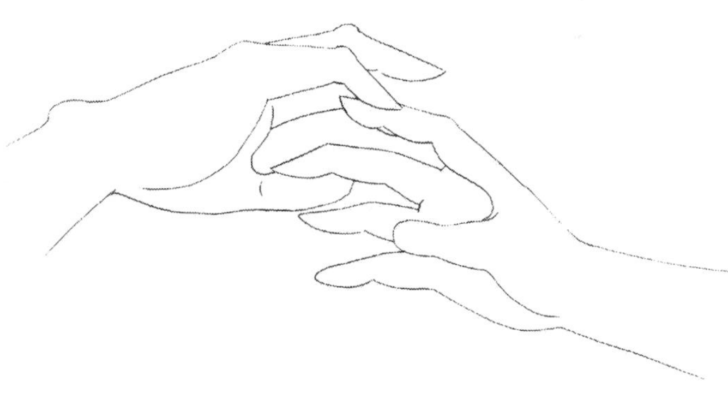

may the best deceiver win

I am poisoned by your lies
but addicted to your sighs

My mind laughs
and my heart cries

because you're the one I'm fond of,
but you're also the one I despise

Sanity is overrated
Our mad love is much more sophisticated

~ Tea Party ~

Come sip some tea
Just you and me.

We'll pour our thoughts out
and let them steam,
talk about our childhood,
and our dreams

Together, we'll laugh and cry
to cover the pain

Life is fun when you're slightly insane

Tough and serious,
with the sharpest jawline I have ever seen

You have that classic look
even with your smooth hair pushed back clean

Is this reality
or just a movie scene?

Soft and sweet inside,
I can see it in your eyes

Is this really how it looks?

I thought this type of love
only lived
in the pages of books

We're both butterflies
in a bee hive

Trapped in danger
Hope we end up alive

As long as you
end up being my king,
I'll take
any bee sting

Whether I look at a flower
or a blank canvas,
your face covers its surface
My mind paints you everywhere I go

I cannot concentrate

I feel like a new born baby
but instead of rock my cradle,
you shake my fate

I am addicted to your sound

With a beat so loud,
it shakes my ground

You're my favorite song
and I can't help but sing along

Constantly playing in my head
Replaying
over and over
until I'm sick of it
and want no more

Don't get too close to me

I'm
warning
you

I'll push you away
but expect you to stay

And it was at that moment that

Your eyes told me a million words
But your lips only spoke one–

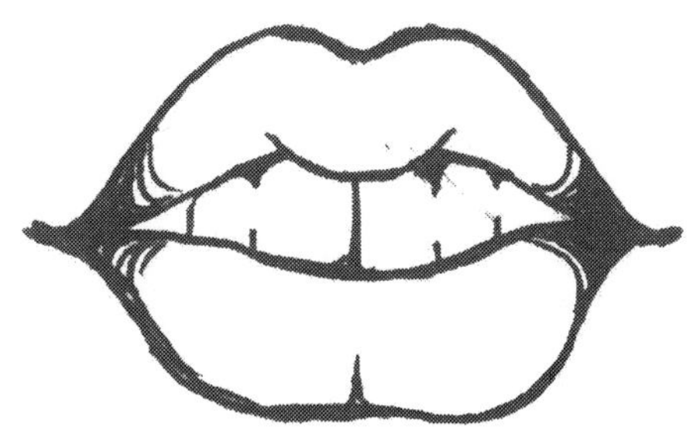

" G o o d b y e "

TOXIC

Shampoo
For Damaged Hair

TOXIC

Shampoo

For Damaged Hair

- Suits the needs for abused hair
- Repairs extreme damage
- Harmful to the eyes
- Guaranteed tears

WARNING: Do not use for too long. Implications may be toxic and harmful to the human soul.

I had a nightmare last night
I lost my vision,
they stole my sight

There were thousands of whispers, I recall
Demons on my back,
they would crawl

A voice takes over my head,
a permanent scream

My mother said,
it's just a ***dream***

Your eyes scream the truth
But your lips are locked by fear

I want to smoke you
and feel you deep in my lungs

Crazy and young,
I taste the ashes on my tongue

Breathing heavy through the pain
until the euphoria
floods into my veins

Even when I quit,
every
breath
is a reminder
of the pain you brought
that made me an addict

Music became my drug

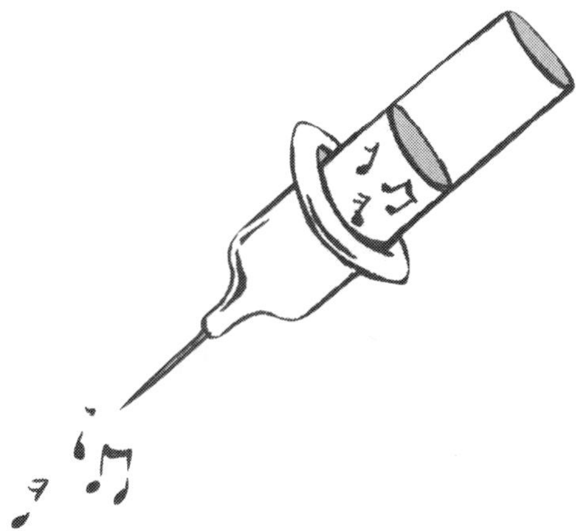

I injected melodies to numb myself
from the poisonous venom
of overthinking

Running from my own mind,
the battle is against me

Drowning in doubts
Sinking in fears
Choked by lies

My mind is occupied
and my thoughts multiply

All I can do now is try
not to cry
and rise

barely above the surface

I find it quite funny
that you cry
at the touch of a sword

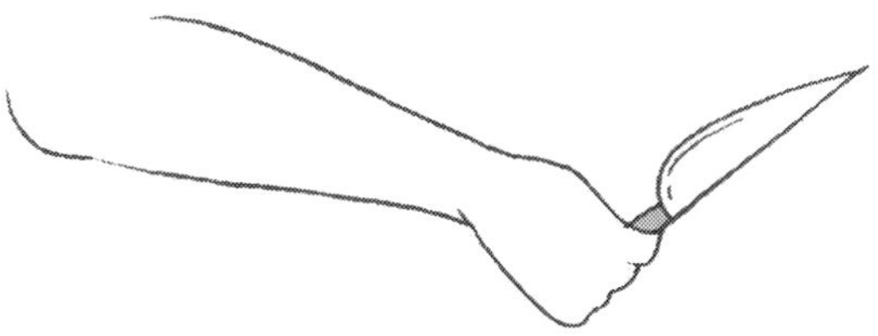

when I became numb
from the thousands
you stuck in my heart

Trust me,

I'm lying

I hate your love

I want you here,

away from me

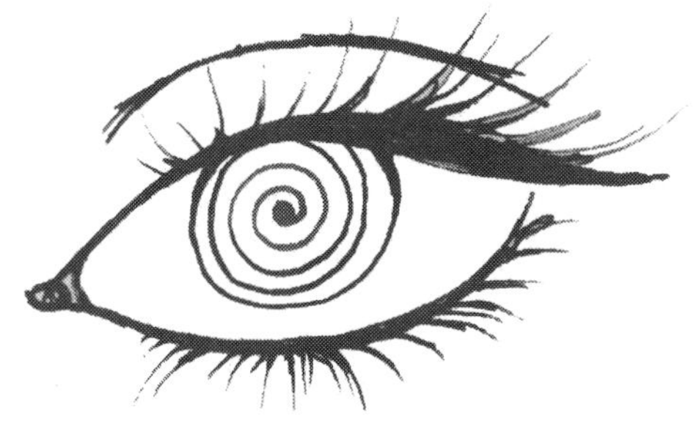

I've lost the ability to think

You threw me down the drain

like the dirty detergent

in your sink

Disorganized thoughts fill my head

Keep thinking about
what I should have said

I think I surpassed my expiration date
Everything came falling down,
so quick..
I guess it's just too late

I still can't accept this to be our fate.

I can't even explain why
that every time I think of you,
I want to cry

How can one be so
heartless,
cold and dry?

Is this some sick kind of test?
You left me in the darkness
I feel a thousand tons
weighing on my chest

I want my happiness back
My breath is waning
I'm having a heart attack

I cannot fathom what you put me through

I cannot wait to see you in this position, too.

I can smell the toxic smoke
There's a fire burning inside of me

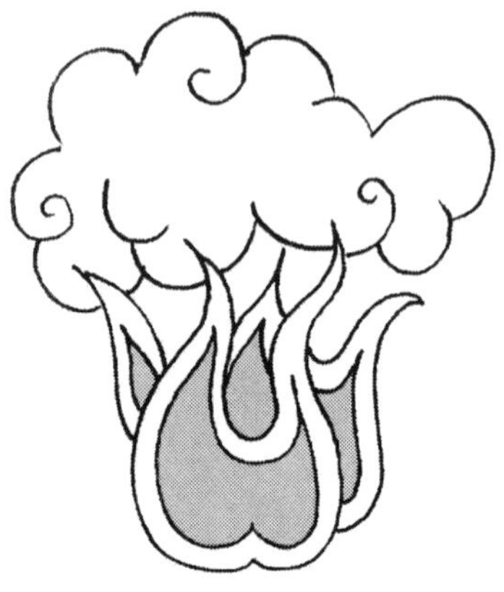

I'm choking
on words
that I shouldn't have spoke

I'm nothing but a liar
Making myself feel like I did right
when everything
has gone haywire

I'm tortured by these decisions
that I regret

I wish we had *never ever* met.

Inject the melodies
in my vein

The rhythm
The beats
All numb my pain

I turn the volume
higher and higher
and shut the world off

until I can no longer feel
the burning fire
of silence
that consumed my soul

I came

tumbling

tumbling

tumbling

down

Fell down to rock bottom,

and didn't even make a sound

Maybe I was saved

or maybe I was found

My heart's crushed,

my mind's off track,

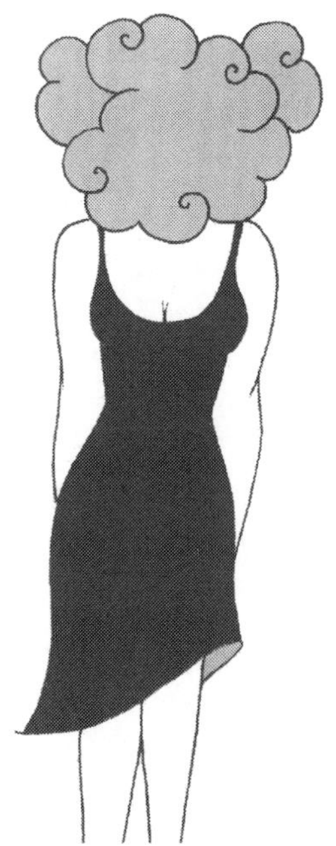

and my soul got lost at the battleground

"Where are we going?"
I would cry

"I see no destination but I like the ride"
I just hope
I'm not the victim of cyanide

The poison is born
in a broken heart

Life has numerous cycles and
this is
just one part

I drank the poison of your soul
because I ran out of my own

Oh, how tragic
it is that
I tasted your toxic affection

Now when you look into my eyes,
I know you want to see
that my heart
has a hole

but it doesn't

My heart is no longer alive
It has condensed into
into a cold, hard stone

She tried to go to sleep
but her stomach was tied in a knot

Turning and tumbling around,
she was dead inside

only considered alive
by the sound
of her
h e a r t b e a t

I see you looking at me now
It's too late though
You want to catch a train
Leading to the past

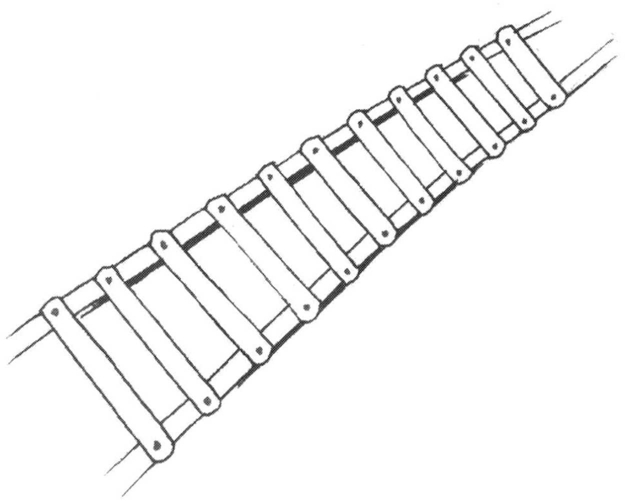

Where I died on the tracks

I inhale your promises
Exhale your lies

Numb and toxic
You've left me paralyzed

I'm the cigar
You're the smoke
I breathe out all the lovely lies you spoke

She was exceptionally smart,
had intellectual interests,
and an appreciation for art

but for him, she lost her mind

For him,
she forgot her worth

For him,
she became blind

My core,
so empty

There lives ***a void***

I used to have one

until it got destroyed

You played with my heart

and messed with my mind

Only to find out that

My soul is the coach
and it's one of a kind

Detangler

Detangler

- Releases tension in the soul
- Gets rid of knots in the hair
- Gently removes preceding pain
- Nourishes heart, soul, and hair

WARNING: Be patient with knots.
Releasing knots is a painful process.

Kill me with knowledge
Burn me with truth
Bury me with understanding

For I'd rather die
knowing what's cruel,
than live as a happy, ignorant fool

I used to look
for happiness
in the melodies of chirping birds

Until I found out that

I was the bird

waiting to ***sing***

For the longest time, I was blind

Sprinting miles
in the dark clouds
with unclear sight

Exhausted,
out of breath,
and out of mind

I ran from
the essence of me

I ran from
what I denied to see

The fountain of truth,
a hidden reality

I sought myself
in distant lands

I was lost
and could not understand

The darkness I saw
gave truth to the light ahead

I had left all the signs and messages unread

As the sun rose above the ocean's horizon,
I was saved from drowning

It took a while

but now I know
how to swim
with the current's flow

It had been a while since our last interaction
Somehow,
I thought revenge
would give me satisfaction

I realized that the pain you caused me
is over now

Your heart may be cold
but my heart only shines gold

I forgive you
for all you have done

Washing away tension,
I'm just having fun

I no longer wish to hide
I no longer wish to run
I sit and watch the clouds move now,
harmonizing with the golden sun

I've found my wings and I'm about to fly
Forgiveness let me soar this high

I pray for you to feel the same

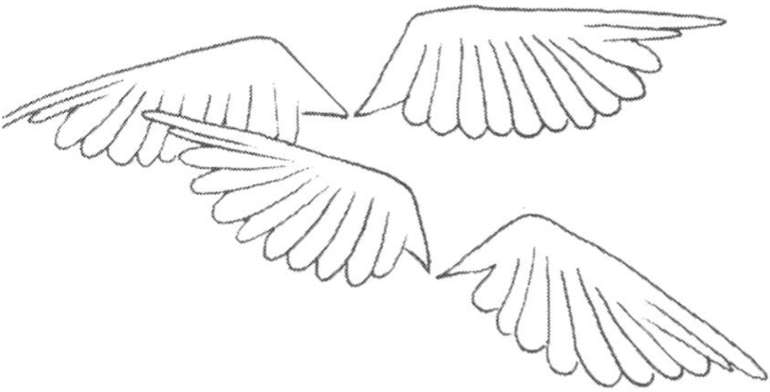

Our hearts are free
Our souls, untamed

Jumped on a train,
I even changed my name

I hid my miserable little frown
I want renewal now
Get me away from this repulsive town

The angst fills my chest
That's it.
I've had enough.
I'm flying away from the nest.

Im chasing my dreams
Watch me,
I'll be the ***b e s t***

I used to surround myself
with noise
because it hid reality

Now I love silence

because I am the *real me*

My life is a polaroid picture
with no contrast

Why is it that
when I want to run forward,
I'm being pulled back
by the past?

But honey,

Don't forget that
polaroid pictures
get pretty with patience

Give it a few seconds

You'll have definition,
brightness,
and saturation

You're just processing
and this phase is ***maturation***

The picture is not developed
It's incomplete

So go on,
keep living,
proceed

Don't let anything in the way impede

This is the only way to succeed

The positive thoughts are
the only ones
you need to feed

Shake it out,
Wait it out

Everything will fall into place
Beyond any doubt

I ran toward the drought
for a drop of water

Even though I'm a child of God,
The universe's daughter

I ran away from what fed me
I chased what starved me
Only God could heal me

I can finally crack a smile
and it's honestly been a while

Life put me in many painful trials

I have dealt with
sorrow,
heartbreak,
and denial

All I sought was a grand revival
so I made choices that
led to my ultimate survival

I took control and
owned my strong will

The universe gave me feelings
nothing else could fulfill

My heart is safe now
in a place, so serene

Now I know what it all was supposed to mean

The universe operates in its own way
Plans get destroyed
and surprises pop up,
unexpected

You must follow the path
in which you are directed

Don't let those clear signs be neglected

The hardest part is
resisting a warm blanket
in the freezing snow

But you must resist temptation
in order to grow

Never apologize
for being yourself

It's not your fault
that people can't handle you

Breathing in hope
Saved by my conscience

Freed by letting go
The only thing stopping me was *nonsense*.

I know that
you think I'm insane
But I'm a lion in a circus
and I have to train

I'm suffering because
they've got me on a heavy chain
and even when I'm in massive pain,
I keep quiet
I don't complain

There's no need to explain what won't sustain

They can temporarily take away my freedom
But they can never
take away my mane

I'm aspiring to feed, not eat
Yeah, I know
I'm pretty neat

So please, doll,
Take a seat
Relax your little princess feet

I've done this before in my sleep
Now, I just have to ***rinse and repeat***

Watching the beautiful clouds
gracefully passing by

I realize that
I owe them an apology

They were here all along
greeting me unconditionally

When I was too blind to notice
or when I lost my focus

They were always watching and protecting me
from above

This moment.
right here
marks our youth

It marks a point
in
endless
time.

This is where
our past meets our future
as we breathe in our legacy

Inhale a second of hope
Exhale a lifetime of fears

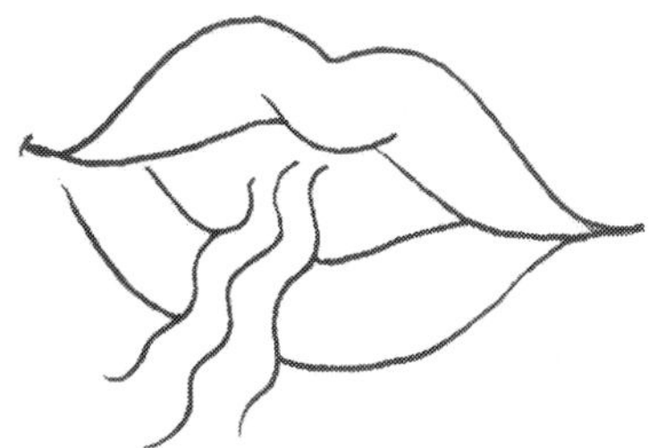

When the sun rises
We all walk along
the same pathways

Some of us stay
buried in shadows of yesterday
and cry in misery
before the day has begun

Some of us walk away
from the darkness
and begin to run
toward the radiating sun

And she walked along the same path
that she used to walk every day
but she could not recognize it
for she had changed
since then

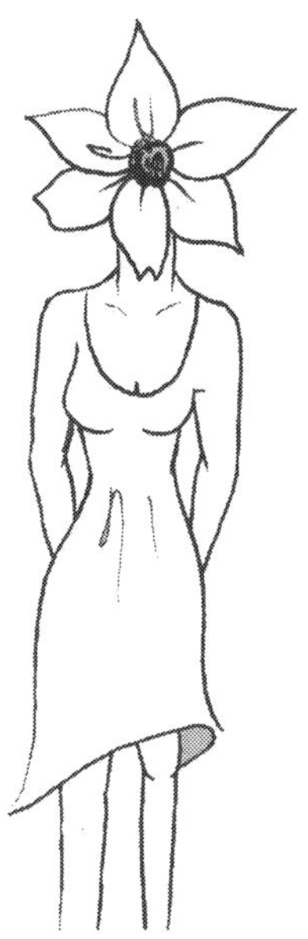

Realizing that we cannot control the thunder
allows us
to embrace the lightning

The sunshine is only beautiful
because of the rainy clouds
that precede it

She realized
after a long time
that his apology
was not necessary
for her forgiveness

You achieve freedom
when you free yourself
from expectations of waiting
and live the exciting life
you were born to live

Couldn't look me in the eyes,
I should have seen the lies
Fast forward to my heart's demise

But then
I saw the need
to change,
grow,
and revise

Because of you,
now I'm wise

Because of myself,
now my heart flies

Doubts are
the seeds of self-destruction

We must boldly conquer every doubt
even when we cannot
figure something out

Confrontation may be hard
especially when it's
you against yourself

You can't cheat her
She's a woman with pride
and God is on her side

After all you did,
the world knows you lied

All those nights,
when she cried,
all you did was hide

even when she went out of her way
for you
and tried

But somewhere through the thundering storm,
She woke up

Instead of looking down
She grew into a queen
and earned a crown
You have *no permission* to make her frown

She's found something more valuable
And that's her ***own sound***
You're here but it's too late now,
so go home
or bow down

Before you leave,
there is something you must know

I'm free now
You cannot touch me

I'm no longer filled with your love,
I'm no longer empty

The universe fills me up
internally

I see light from inside
and my soul shines,
worldwide

I mourn our times together

For now,
I've become wise

And looking back with eyes so wide,
I cannot trust those lovely lies

Shampoo for Extra Shine

Shampoo for Extra Shine

- For strong and healthy hair
- Gives hair a beautiful, radiant glow
- Strengthens the soul's sense of individuality and courage

WARNING: None.

Ugly sounds, pretty voices

The words we speak define our choices

What we send
is what we receive

The person in the mirror
is the one you must believe

A man approached her from afar
He told her to shut up
and get in the car

Wise girl she was,
she walked away

She asked God to help him,
she knew the best thing to do
was pray

He came again,
trying to buy her
with jewelry, so nice

She rolled her eyes

and didn't look twice

because

she was the jewel

She knew her time was precious

and it had no price

Her ambition broke walls

Her voice liberated fears

Her smile invited positivity

No one understood

how her mind was wired

She dreamt of a world

that she inspired

Laugh loudly,
play silly,
and jump around,
with no shame

Constantly evolving,
we only worry about
remaining the same

This life is an adventurous game
and there is no structured frame

Forget the norm

Be ***you***

in your purest form

I focused on the minute
and lost the hour

I lost momentum
but I gained more power

Through pain,
my soul grew so strong

With love,
my soul knew no wrong

Looking inside,
I found a seed
on the floor
of my core

I watered it with passion,
patience galore

Grew a forest
where abundance poured

Since I stopped
looking at the clock,
more than one bird came

It was the entire flock

I sat silent…

and let life come to talk

We live deep in the ocean
We rule the entire sea
We invite you to join our community

Our pain and worries float to the surface
Under water,
we find our purpose

This is where the soul can thrive
Purity of Water takes over,
the vicious Fire can't survive

No violence
We embrace life
We have swordfish,
and don't need a knife
Nothing can stop us
We have harmony

Our souls swim
courageous, wild, and free

Don't look too far ahead

We were made to enjoy

what lays right in front of us

Go out on your rooftop
and sing as loud as you can

Dance in public
as if you were alone

Your persona has sound
so make it
l o u d
and everyone will come around

Make the world dance
to the music of your soul

We all add one piece
to make this beautiful world
whole

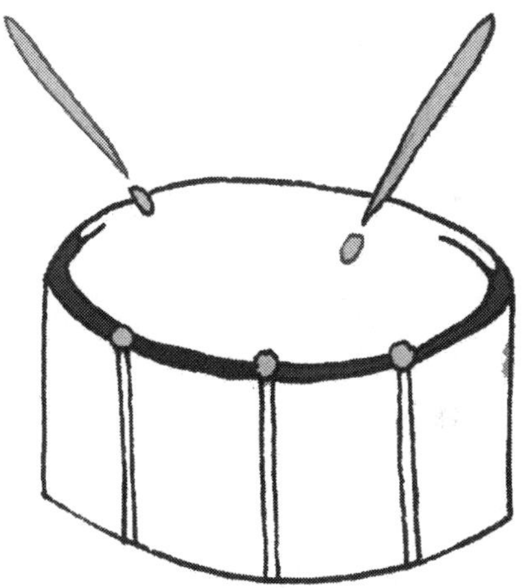

The sun may cast
a different shadow
on you than on me

and that's okay

But the rays of light
are of the same source
United by the door of the universe,
peace is the key

Let life take its course

Infatuate me with intellect
Charm me with knowledge
And enlighten my soul with wisdom
Then, you shall earn my respect

You looked for love in
a charming smile
and dreamy eyes

You even spent the day
to fantasize
and justify those irrelevant lies

Sitting still,
you continuously waited

but you failed to see that

you are your own soulmate

Don't worry, love

They might laugh at you for standing out

but you're a beautiful flower
in a garden full of seeds
that have not sprout

She radiates gracefully
She's one of a kind,
with her unique personality,
and her beautiful mind

She wears a white dress
Simple, elegant, comfortable
She has no one to impress

That's what makes her strong
Standing bold
without validation,
She can never be wrong

She's in a gallery
for the world to see

Only, she doesn't fit
in a standard frame

She's a masterpiece.

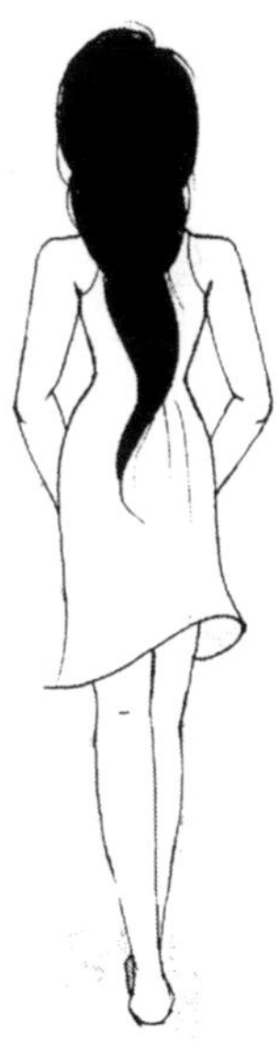

Life has its tough times
Sometimes we have to jump hurdles,
oh so tall

and I hate to tell you, doll
but there is no magic wand...

The only power lies
in the way that you respond

She wore makeup
because she wanted to

She glowed
because she was born to

She was a fighter
because she was destined to be

She spoke her mind
because she was brave

She only did it for herself
so darling,
don't flatter yourself

She's a library,
and you're just another book on the shelf

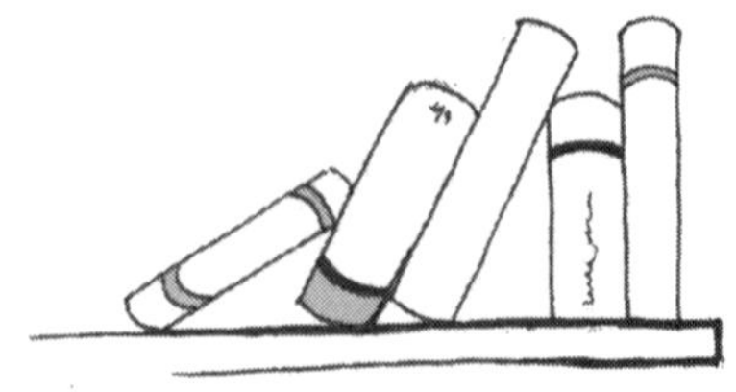

No one could compete with her
No one was the same

The world saw her beauty as a crime
But all she wanted to do was shine

Be grateful
for a drop of water
and you will
receive the ocean

Expect the ocean
and you won't even get
a drop of water

They call us insane

We laugh at their pathetic reality

We created this mentality

Darling,

you just got an ugly personality

You have nothing to prove to them
You are much more than what they see

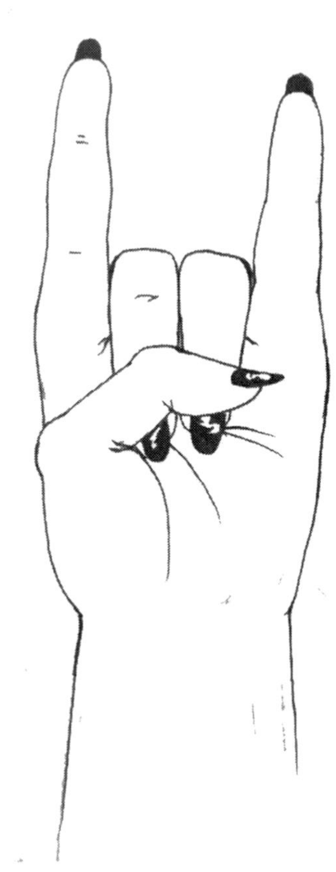

Make the world move

Shake the entire sea

And once the music plays
everyone rejoices
to the beautiful sounds
around them

The eyes gain sight into
a new world
where everyone
radiates the unique
positivity of human nature

United by the love
for a vibrant source of energy
in the form of sound

The music flows
and everyone glows

Don't be scared

Just be prepared

Remove negativity and
avoid the confusion

Fear is nothing
but a silly illusion

Him
Her
He
She
Why does it matter?

We are all born free
to be anyone we want to be

Regardless of

color,

interests,

height,

size,

name,

or gender

Be yourself

Find your center

A gusty wind
may tremble your leaves
and even your strong and sturdy branches

But
the shaking,
the breaking,
that's all around
cannot affect your deep roots in the ground

She saw no competition,
Or any little contradiction

Her view was simple.
Everyone had their own journey

Possessed a soul so abundant,
and a heart so generous,

She made the world move
in continuous harmony

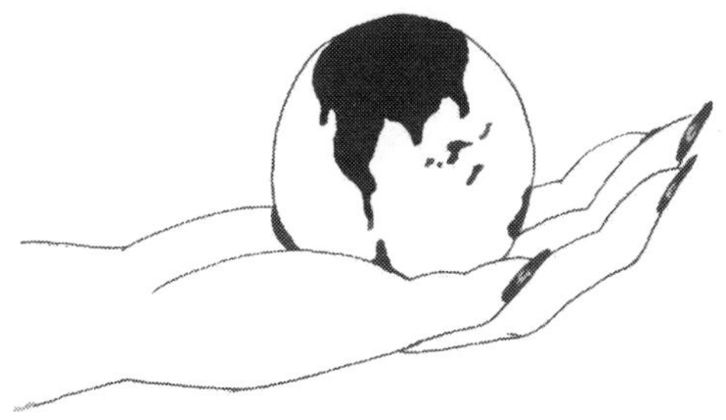

She knew no boundaries
and spoke the truth
despite harsh circumstances

Down to earth and sincere,
bold yet courteous,
dangerous yet lovely,
radiating with joy and kindness,
The world was in her hands

Her spirit alive at earth's core,
Uniting humanity with her soul

Her smile was even present
at the North and South Pole

And when things would take a toll,
she persevered until she achieved her goal

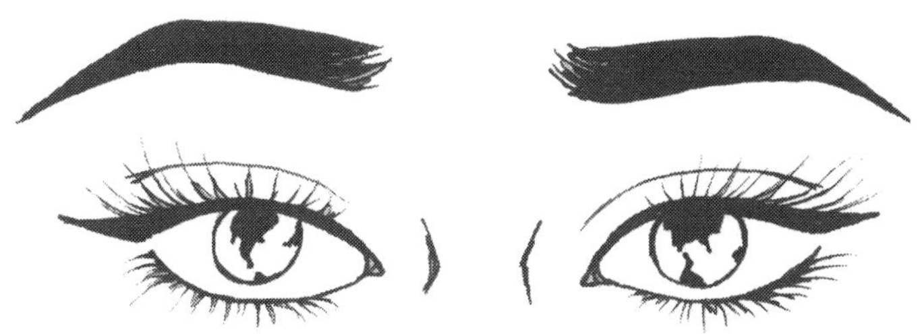

The forecast shows cloudy
with a chance of fright

I'm not afraid though,
I was born to fight
My muscles get hard
and my body gets tight

Im prepared for this
And I know that
I won't miss

Here I go!
Watch this punch
I'm about to throw

It's raining victory
and I'm drenched
In fact, I'm soaking wet.

Believing that there were challenges that I
couldn't defeat?
That's the only thing I regret

There was even
a ten percent chance of terror

But I know my role
as the universe's light bearer

What if I told you
that every second of your life
is orchestrated
so perfectly
and purposefully

And that you are supposed
to be exactly here
at this very moment
and any other situation
would not be right

The world around her
told her that
she was worth nothing

But the universe
inside her soul showed her that
she *was* everything

The sun came back to life
as she walked into the room

Her confident presence
in perfect synergy
with the rays of sunshine

She wore controversy
on her eyelashes
and danger on her lips

Her soul gave birth to innovation
and her energy built an entire nation

The look in her eyes
Screamed ,

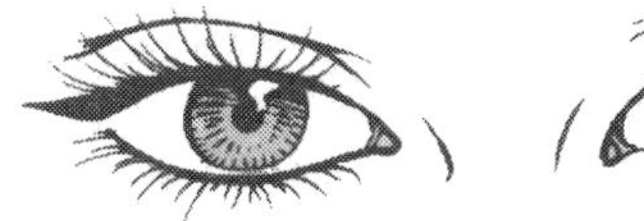

"There is nothing I can't handle"

She radiated
the sun's light
with a heart so brave

After all,
she was a diamond
glistening in the light
with shine so effortless
and beauty so genuine

Everyone wanted her sparkle
but didn't see
the past that shaped
her perfect curves and edges
that formed her glow

She looks at the ground
so innocently
like an angel

but do not
underestimate her

She's a tiger
maintaining a calm composure
before she goes to hunt

She'll eat your mind
and claw your soul out
before you can even shout

Next time,
when you see that a girl is quiet,
Leave a little doubt

You have *no idea* what she's about

There is no such thing as a mistake
or a failure

We are destined to constantly learn
and evolve
and cultivate with wisdom

Ask yourself,
what could be more perfect than that?

Seek the energy that
you want to be

Our thoughts become who we are

The power of imagination
takes impossible ideas
And makes reality change to fit them

That is why you must wholeheartedly
believe in your ingenious ideas,
inventive spirit,
and courageous soul

Your individuality is your greatest asset, love

Expand your horizons
Take the risks that will lead to your growth
and most importantly,

♫ *Find your own sound* ♫

There is nothing in the world
that can compare
to the brilliant music of your soul

Wash your hair.

Cleanse your soul.

Use Shampoo ❤

I cannot express my gratitude in words for having you join me throughout this soul-cleansing process.

Thank you for your patience and abundant love.

Our most challenging endeavors require us to endure pain,
but reward us with valuable wisdom.

I hope that your hair eternally shines as bright as your soul and individuality.

\- Ariel Sara R.

To maintain a clean & healthy soul,

Stay connected

~ Join the movement ~

Take a picture of your favorite page and tag the accounts below

Feel free to use #Shampoo

Twitter: @ArielSaraR

Instagram: @ArielSaraR

Facebook: Facebook.com/ArielSaraR

Snapchat: @ArielSaraR

Official website: ArielSaraR.com

Thank you

About The Author

ARIEL SARA R.

is a poet based in the Greater Los Angeles area.

From a young age, Ariel exposed herself to the therapeutic elements of music and poetry. She gradually began to recognize the powerful relationship between song lyrics, music, poetry, and art in connecting to the human soul.

In addition, Ariel viewed art as a medium for unity among individuals. Today, Ariel sees art–of all kinds– to nurture the individuality of one's soul.

Thus, she created ***Shampoo*** to spark a movement towards empowering individual strength and embracing one's unique sound.

Moving forward, Ariel aspires to bring individuals and communities together with the harmonizing power of art and expression.

Made in the USA
San Bernardino, CA
05 December 2016